MALCOLM X

M A L C

The Great

Photographs

O L M X

Text by

Thulani Davis

Photographs researched

and edited by

Howard Chapnick

Stewart
Tabori
& Chang
New York

Page 1: 1964 (John Launois/
Black Star).
Pages 2 and 3: 1963 (Gordon Parks).
Page 5: Malcolm X speaking
(Susan Kellogg).

Published in 1993 by
Stewart, Tabori & Chang, Inc.
575 Broadway
New York, New York 10012

LIBRARY OF CONGRESS
CATALOGING-IN-PUBLICATION DATA
Davis, Thulani.
Malcolm X : the great photographs /
by Thulani Davis ; photographs
researched and edited by
Howard Chapnick.
Includes bibliographical references
and index.
ISBN 1-55670-312-0
ISBN 1-55670-317-1 (paperback)
1. X, Malcolm, 1925–1965—
Pictorial works.   2. Black Muslims—
Biography—Pictorial works.
3. Afro-Americans—biography—
Pictorial works.   I. Chapnick,
Howard.   II. Title.
BP223.Z8L57333   1993
320.5'4'092—dc20   92-32643
[B]   CIP

2654 7541

Distributed in the U.S. by
Workman Publishing
708 Broadway
New York, New York 10003

Distributed in Canada by
Canadian Manda Group
P.O. Box 920 Station U
Toronto, Ontario M8Z 5P9

Distributed in all other territories
(except Central and South America)
by Melia Publishing Services,
P.O. Box 1639, Maidenhead,
Berkshire SL6 6YZ England

Central and South American accounts
should contact Export Sales Manager,
Stewart, Tabori & Chang.

Printed in Japan
10 9 8 7 6 5 4 3 2

CONTENTS

The name and face of Malcolm X are at this moment probably more widely known than they were at his death in 1965. His face has become an omnipresent icon, a silent image attracting people who bring to it their ideas of Malcolm. People attach to him concepts like power, solidarity within the national African-American community, self-empowerment, group empowerment, rebellion, and the ultimate refusal to join, to assimilate, or to be placated. **D**epending on who is looking, the face of Malcolm X, or El-Hajj Malik El-Shabazz, conjures up various men: moral leader, nationalist leader, black separatist leader, Black Muslim teacher, radical leader, pan-Africanist leader, pioneer in the spread of orthodox Islam. Some will see a demagogue, or self-indulgent renegade. Some will see a face they once hated and may have come to respect. **E**ven the letter *X* transforms in association with Malcolm. X is used in Western culture to signify an unknown quantity or force, and the letter was once a fixture in science fiction, denoting futuristic technological developments—X rays, X-guns, X-men. The Nation of Islam, also known as the Black Muslims, used the X to make a political point. An X replacing the last name among Muslims represented a fact most African-Americans then knew but did not discuss—as individuals and families we did not and probably could not know our original family names, which had been stripped from the Africans brought here in slavery. The X brought home a point that would lead many, like Alex Haley, to ask the question, Can we ever hope to find out our specific histories? **I**n the 1990s, X has come to signify simply one man who wore that surname: Malcolm. X, the ultimate reduction of all Malcolm's words and ideas, has become a symbol, a badge of belonging and a sign of cash sales. His presence everywhere we look also seems inescapably to be a statement of longing, a wish being made known on city streets. **I**n an age without visible, significant leaders, his mute image, newly hip in every detail from horn-rimmed glasses to stingy brim hat, trim goatee, and plain white shirt, means much to many who do not have his gift for communication, who never saw him "work" an audience or throw down one of his amazing mixes of blunt spade-calling, dazzling political analysis, and instantly enlightening motherwit. Some of those who heard him in the 1960s recall that he stood out because he specifically addressed black people, not all of America. This caught their interest because many of our leaders were jockeying for a place in a national forum. Many young blacks today are in the same situation, living in an age in which even community-based leaders communicate through the electronic media and therefore tailor their remarks to the larger white audience. Who speaks directly to them? The face, image, likeness of a man who last stood before an audience nearly thirty years ago.

Malcolm X's enormous popularity now lies in the resilience of his myth and in our own need for such a myth more than in the teaching and understanding of his work. Despite the wealth of information coming out these days about the man's life, the myth of a man transformed by his own efforts still looms larger than any facts or dates.

Malcolm X was himself the originator of this tale of transformation and, long before he became widely known, he used the mythic aspects of his own life as a tool with which to teach. "I finished the eighth grade in Mason, Michigan," he used to tell audiences. "My high school was the black ghetto of Roxbury. My college was the streets of Harlem. And my master's was taken in prison." He could say, in so many words, "You've heard my story—if the teachings of the Honorable Elijah Muhammad could raise me up, open my eyes, then surely it can help us all." This is not an exact quote, but it is the method he used from the earliest days of his ministry following his conversion and release from prison.

The story of Malcolm's early life, as he told it, galvanized people who'd had similar experiences or who were fascinated by the contrast between the traumatic childhood he described and the supremely self-confident, articulate man who stood before them. Telling the life story is a strategy as old as the black experience in America, and it has been used as a political tool from the time of the antislavery movement to the present. Escaped slaves were once sent on tours of the North to organize whites against slavery, and in 1964 Fannie Lou Hamer, a former sharecropper from Mississippi, riveted the nation by telling the story of her life at the Democratic con-

Page 6: 1964 (John Launois/Black Star)

8

vention as black Mississippians struggled to use their right to vote. But many of those stories have become part of our heritage, even part of our triumph. Malcolm's story goes on as a painful reminder of the ways in which we continue to suffer. For those who live his story, victory has not yet been won.

1960 (Robert L. Haggins)

It is a cruel reality that today all the elements of Malcolm's narrative are much more common than when he told it. It is the story of the breakup of a family by social-service agencies following his father's death, his discouragement by a teacher after he finished at the top of his class, his impression that the hustler's life was a smarter path for a young black man who had so few options for survival. Malcolm talked about his drug addiction, arrest, conviction, and imprisonment. That experience is as common today as tales of beating, starvation, and abuse were in the days of slavery. It is typical of the black urban male's story in countless news reports and in a numbing number of fictional television and film entertainments. Malcolm's life as Malcolm Little is the slave narrative of the twentieth century.

The story of Malcolm's life after his conversion to the Nation of Islam while in prison is less commonly told in popular culture. The public still learns very little about the religious organization that gave him the name Malcolm X and provided him with the training to recruit and organize people and to edit and distribute a newspaper. The Nation of Islam was, of course, not the only black organization that changed and trained people. But the stories we see and hear are of individuals overcoming the odds, not of communities working as one mind. This is how American stories are told, how the 1960s are retold, and is one reason people continue to evaluate their times in terms of the presence of strong leaders rather than strong communities.

We have yet to see the stories of the Garvey movement, for instance, to which Malcolm's parents belonged. Garvey's idea of a black self-help group based on some of Booker T. Washington's accomplishments grew into a mass movement promoting black nationalism, ties to Africa (which influenced the early black movements in South Africa), and black self-determination all over the globe. (Malcolm's mother, Louise Little, not only wrote articles for Garvey's newspaper *The Negro World* but sometimes translated *World* articles into several other languages. It's not hard to see how the Nation of Islam became attractive to Malcolm and other members of his family, given their Garveyite background.) And of course, there are other stories we have not seen: the students of the Student Nonviolent Coordinating Committee on the southern front lines, or the black people of Albany, Georgia, who were jailed en masse during Malcolm's time.

In Malcolm's case, the Nation of Islam is important because it defined his early public presence. The Nation, a separatist group that espoused the idea of a black nation within the bounds of the United States, sent him around the country to urban black communities and gave him the conviction and beliefs that grounded his initial political thinking.

While many then found the separatist idea repellent, the very notion of an African-American community remaining apart by choice not only forced Malcolm into a unique place among black leaders but led him to *think* about all the issues in terms quite different from his peers among the civil-rights leaders. The emphasis on self-sufficiency was at the heart of this difference, perhaps explaining the Nation of Islam's success at developing programs for the treatment of drug addiction in our communities; it also was one of the first groups since Reconstruction to develop programs aimed, for better or worse, at shoring up the embattled black family. Islam as practiced by the Nation was quite different from orthodox Islam as we know it, but those who adapted Islamic ideas to suit the black American situation coincidentally encouraged interest in African cultures and societies.

While Malcolm's early life story parallels those of others who survived societal brutality and went on to serve a community in distress, Malcolm's departure from the Nation, and his second conversion to a larger world view on his visit to Mecca, is a chapter taken from many classical stories, tales in which a person is granted by the eternal spirit a vision of humanity's infinite possibilities.

Malcolm's last few years are part of a tragic portrait of America's violent history. The Nation of Islam's turn against him, the constant surveillance by government agencies, and the threats against his life are facts we understand today from the experience of many black leaders in the 1960s. Malcolm's murder took place in an environment of known threat, and yet there was no visible police presence in the Audubon Ballroom where he was killed. This fact, which seemed shocking at the time, as well as the later revelation that the "bodyguard" who tried to resuscitate him was an undercover New York City police officer, no longer even seem remarkable. In spring 1992, as Los Angeles went up in flames, we could see buildings burn unattended on our TVs; we could hear officials ordering police and firemen not to bother.

El-Hajj Malik El-Shabazz's murder, as he attempted to focus his political work and solidify both an Islamic group (Muslim Mosque, Inc.) and a human rights organization (Organization of Afro-American Unity, or OAAU), places him in a tragic lineage—leadership cut down in a struggle over the power of ideas. The assassination of people whose chief power is a compelling set of ideas, rather than state power or armies, happens in every society. In this society, though, where the legacies of slavery live on with such vigor, the assassination of a national leader, or of a local activist, will continue to have the effect of a lynching. In the 1960s many were cut down, among them Malcolm X, Rev. Martin Luther King, Jr., Medgar

Evers, Jimmie Lee Jackson, Fred Hampton, Andrew Goodman, Michael Schwerner, and James Chaney. They don't become Gandhis; they join a long line of lynching victims.

The story, both real and mythic, lives and grows. Malcolm's book, *The Autobiography of Malcolm X*, is being read by young African-Americans who'd never heard of him ten years ago and have learned of him recently through popular mass products, as well as college-educated people—black and white—who grew up hearing his name associated with black race hatred and violence. (I knew the book had reached true street-level hit status when I was in a bookstore and a brother next to me lifted ten or more copies of it, put them under his jacket, and ran out the door. Things still being like they were when Malcolm was alive, when they caught the cat outside I froze in place, expecting to be collared and searched as well.)

Like other icons, Malcolm has been the subject of treatments in all the art forms. There are paintings of Malcolm, from traditional heroic renderings by Nelson Stevens to risky polemical works by Sue Coe. There are countless street murals. Among the poems are heavies by Amiri Baraka and David Henderson. Rap artists use samplings from his recorded speeches, and his loss is mourned in the elegiac "Malcolm, Malcolm, Semper Malcolm" on jazz artist Archie Shepp's 1965 *Fire Music*. There are several film and television documentaries on Malcolm, and at least four plays: *Chickens Come Home to Roost*, by Laurence Holder (a fictional setting of the last confrontation with Elijah Muhammad, in which Denzel Washington originated the role of Malcolm); *The Meeting*, by Jeff Stetson (a fictional meeting between Malcolm and Martin Luther King, Jr.); two with the title *El-Hajj Malik El-Shabazz*, one by Barbara Ann Teer, one by M. R. Davidson, Jr.; and I co-wrote an opera with Anthony Davis, *X (The Life and Times of Malcolm X)*. Undoubtedly the most widely seen work on his life will be *Malcolm X*, the film made by Spike Lee.

If we want to think about why Malcolm as an image has so much currency today, it helps to look beyond the myths at some of those ideas and how they have transformed people. A. Peter Bailey, a member of the OAAU who knew Malcolm during the last two years of his life, best sums up Malcolm's legacy: Malcolm "left behind *minds*." Bailey calls Malcolm "a master teacher":

[Malcolm] used to always say 'The Revolution we need is a revolution of the mind.' He was the kind of person that once you heard

him, even if you disagreed with him, you could never go back to thinking the way you were before you heard him. He literally compelled you to check yourself out, and check out your beliefs. But you never could go back to where you were before you heard him.

Nowadays we would have to liken his verbal agility to the masterful moves of Michael Jordan. He was deft in his analysis and "def" in his use of the language, adding terms to the black vernacular like "tricknology"—which you can tell by looking is a brief way of describing systemic b.s. In 1964 he was telling us we were African-Americans:

That's what we are—Africans who are in America. . . . Nothing but Africans. In fact, you'd get further calling yourself African instead of Negro. Africans don't catch hell. They don't have to pass civil-rights bills for Africans.—"The Ballot or the Bullet"

Malcolm gave us a few lines that need no embellishment: "The cost of freedom is death" (from a television newsreel interview); or "You get your freedom by letting your enemy know that you'll do anything to get your freedom" (from a recording called *The Wisdom of Malcolm X*, EF Records); or "Don't waste your time on [Uncle] Tom, never worry about the puppet, go after the puppeteer." We know what they mean even when abbreviated: "by any means necessary."

Some of Malcolm's harsh wit and even his lexicon no doubt spring from the West Indian tongue of his mother. When, for instance, he talked about the white man being a "thief" who "stole us and then stole our religion, our language, and our civilization and made us into animals," he echoes the witticisms of Caribbean cultures where one could hear the rhetorical question, "If buckra [the white man] no tief, what are we doin' here?"

And he could be very *exacting* about the meaning and power of word. He said there was "a black revolution and a Negro revolution" ("Message to the Grass Roots"). It doesn't take much imagination to guess which one he thought would be put out of business quickly.

Malcolm's agility on the podium was simply the well-tailored clothing that dressed an analysis. His ideas shifted and grew over the years as his thinking broadened and sharpened. Many of his ideas are still useful today because he addressed the situation of African-Americans on three levels:

First, he showed that we face systemic racism, a political structure that fails to serve the lives of African-American people. In March 1964 he said:

Good education, housing, and jobs are imperatives for the Negroes and I shall support them in their fight to win these objectives, but I shall tell the Negroes that while these are necessary, they cannot solve the main Negro problem.

While full citizenship and equal opportunity in education, jobs, transportation, and public facilities were the thrust of the civil-rights movement, Malcolm taught that achieving short-term goals without an analysis of the long-term functioning of government and society would fail to bring about freedom and justice.

Second, unlike many civil-rights leaders who concentrated on institutional reform—integration, voting rights—Malcolm recognized that within African-American communities there were problems that could not be solved by legislation. We must ourselves, he said, be the creative, constructive force that heals, rebuilds, prevents the disintegration of the family and community.

Third, Malcolm was an important public voice calling for a global view. At a time when we were completely absorbed by the daily trials of a movement involved in direct action and a propaganda war in the electronic media, few people looked at the impact of our struggle across the world. Malcolm saw the necessity for expanding the American struggle from "civil rights" to "human rights," advocating, like some of the thinkers and activists before him, that African-Americans develop an international agenda, linking ourselves to those with whom we share understanding, particularly in Africa.

THE SYSTEM

I don't go for any organization—be it civil rights or any other kind—that has to compromise with the power structure . . .
—*Malcolm X, interview on radio station WBAI, January 28, 1965*

"Brother Malcolm was the first one I remember hearing talk about the system," recalls Peter Bailey:

He never said, "It's the George Wallace types." I'd come out of Howard University and I'd been involved in the civil-rights movement. We'd been taught that this was rednecks, po' white trash, an aberration. And Brother Malcolm said, "Oh, no, no, no, no, we're talking about a whole system."

In addition to the stunning events taking place on our televisions during the 1960s, a dialogue was taking place among black leaders. Thinking about the black situation in America became a public activity. Movement strategies and positions shifted weekly, and in a sense we were all part of a national forum in which ideas shared only in kitchens and political-science classrooms were aired in debates, interviews, and newspapers. Malcolm X and James Baldwin stood out among these voices for their uncompromising critique of America.

William Strickland, former director of the Northern Student Movement and now associate professor in the W. E. B. Du Bois Department of Afro-American Studies at the University of Massachusetts, Amherst, recalls:

It was Malcolm and Jimmy [Baldwin] coming together, confirming a totally different view of the white world.

Blacks and whites have a differential relationship to America. Malcolm just capsulized all that in his position about "democracy is hypocrisy." It wasn't just a metaphorical put-down; it captured that concept in fundamental ways. As Malcolm took you through the history from Africa through slavery and hooked it up to the present, you gained the sense that the form may change, the faces may change, the actors may change, but the fundamental relationship to you doesn't change. And it wasn't just the hypocrisy of the white/Western/American history; he was also death on the white liberals, our so-called allies. And every time they would reveal themselves, he was on it like white on rice.

Malcolm's view was well understood in 1964 when "allies" in the Democratic party abandoned the Mississippi Freedom Democratic Party at the Democratic convention in Atlantic City. Mississippi blacks who had never been able to exercise their right to vote came with a delegation to the convention and demonstrated that the all-white Mississippi delegation was unjustly constituted and did not represent the state. Liberal allies of the movement failed to see the blacks recognized. While there are certainly other examples of the failure of liberal support, the events in Atlantic City proved a turning point for many activists.

Malcolm saw that one could easily be distracted by individuals or events, and he kept his eye on the power structure itself. He saw the structure's essential flaw was its racism, and in speaking about it he made the same critique given earlier by black scholar and writer W. E. B. Du Bois: full democracy has never taken place in America. A system that does not allow our participation (despite guarantees written into its very structure) cannot function for us:

You and I in America are faced not with a segregationist conspiracy,

we're faced with a government conspiracy. . . . The same govern-
ment that you go abroad and fight for and die for is the government
that is in a conspiracy to deprive you of your voting rights, deprive
you of your economic opportunities, deprive you of decent housing,
deprive you of decent education. . . . And you should drop it in their

lap. This government has failed the Negro. This so-called democ-
racy has failed the Negro. And all these white liberals have defi-
nitely failed the Negro.—"The Ballot or the Bullet"

He correctly predicted what in fact happened once blacks
came in large numbers into the voting booths in the South
after passage of the Voting Rights Act:

If the black man in these southern states had his full voting rights

. . . the Democratic party itself would lose power. You just can't belong to that party without analyzing it.
—"The Ballot or the Bullet"

The sudden appearance of large numbers of black voters in the South in fact accounted first for politicians like George Wallace changing their campaign stripes from appealing to rednecks to all southerners. But the long-term effect was an abandonment of the party by whites, particularly middle-class males and poor whites, followed by a shift to the right within the party, aping the Republican party, which rose to power after the civil-rights era.

As many in the northern movement were able to see from experience, integration was not going to change a racist system. Malcolm pointed this out:

The Negro revolution . . . is the only revolution in which the goal is a desegregated lunch counter, a desegregated theater, a desegregated park, and a desegregated public toilet.
—"Message to the Grass Roots"

Yet when he saw the brutality meted out to blacks demonstrating in the South—dog attacks, firehose attacks, and even the bombing of a Birmingham church that killed four little girls—he came to champion them. And of course he knew that the southern movement, which did integrate lunch counters, would accomplish change in the South. Still, Malcolm was the reminder that justice is a much larger, much longer struggle, not with stores, businesses, or southern mores but with a political and cultural complex opposed to self-determination.

The mob violence in the South and police brutality in the North brought out many questions among blacks concerning passive resistance and self-defense. King's nonviolent tactics were greatly admired by many, and yet others like Malcolm questioned them. Malcolm believed in self-defense: not just self-defense in the heat of the moment, but as a right:

There is nothing in our book, the Koran, that teaches us to suffer peacefully. Our religion teaches us to be intelligent.
—"Message to the Grass Roots"

There certainly is something in the Christian book about taking the suffering, and instantly we recognized in his language how deeply it ran in our culture.

But of all these insights perhaps the most valuable for this time is Malcolm's understanding that the most important change has to take place in our own minds. People living in a time when the visible movements of the past are dead or diminished often develop the impression that the very inertia of the times will prevent any change from ever taking place. Movement does not take place without an analysis of the history, the moment, and the needs. Change, in society, in people, even in how we receive immutable realities or "acts of God," begins with a change in the human mind.

TAKING CARE OF OUR OWN

You're either part of the problem, or part of the solution.
—*Aaron Henry, Mississippi Freedom Democratic Party*

Even while struggling with issues of power, problems within the African-American community needed to be tackled on several fronts. By 1964 Malcolm taught the need for economic self-determination, a new term then; "we should control the economy of our community" he says in his speech "The Ballot or the Bullet." And he knew too that problems usually handled by "social services" could not be left for someone else to fix.

Malcolm X's experience was significant in developing his positions on "in house" problems among African-Americans. Until recent years the institutions in our communities consistently dealing with black family problems were the churches, but Malcolm's orientation came from a different source. He was grounded in a philosophy that valued the male-headed family, and attempted to train black men and women in both means of financial support and nurturing skills. The Nation of Islam's program had also attempted to move people away from the adoption of the dominant [white] culture that itself was experiencing the disintegration of family and community. In some respects the Muslims were emulating the model of closed immigrant communities, such as the Chinese-American community. A separatist inclination had the effect of forestalling the breakup of families and the adoption of the individualistic orientation of the larger culture. This clinging to traditional values also made those communities more impervious to change, such as the empowerment of women.

Even after his break with the Nation of Islam, Malcolm still reflected on these problems in a way not tackled by most so-called leaders, who preferred to address themselves solely to the national political arena.

We have to get together and remove the evils, the vices, alcoholism, drug addiction, and other evils that are destroying the moral fiber of our community. We ourselves have to lift the level of our

community, . . . make our own society beautiful so that we will be satisfied in our own social circles. . . . Don't change the white man's mind—you can't change his mind, and that whole thing about appealing to the moral conscience of America—America's conscience is bankrupt. . . . So it is not necessary to change the white man's mind. We have to change our own mind.—"The Ballot or the Bullet"

Speaking about the problems in our communities without reference to what the white society must do to address them was largely unheard of in the 1960s. Today we would more likely hear such comments from black conservatives, who have long complained that black leadership expected government to do what black communities have not done. Malcolm, then, cannot simply be lumped into the standard profile of a progressive or radical of his time; he was indeed more complex than that. In speaking about these issues, Malcolm anticipated a turn forced on leaders of the 1990s by realities more harsh than he might have ever imagined.

The Black Muslims did not have a progressive view of women's roles in society, and Malcolm himself never developed a programmatic plan for providing women with greater skills, support, and protections. Elevating us to being "sisters" and "queens" and offering the protection of the community, of modest dress and male partners, would not suffice over the long haul to address structural issues inside families and society. As the recent development of a strong black women's health movement has shown, there is widespread need for work in the areas of domestic violence, poverty, harassment, medical services, and even nutrition. It was said by Ossie Davis, and since by many others, that "Malcolm was our manhood, our living black manhood." This was true for *all* of us— he was the manhood, or powerfulness, of black women too, and he represented a male ideal to many women who were looking for a new model of the black male as life partner, father, community person. Yet that very phrase—"he was our manhood"—points to a struggle then still to come within our understanding of political work.

While I have no doubt that Brother Malcolm would have expanded from his oft-quoted statement that a civilization is only as great as its women to understand issues facing us today, his impact on us then was as a male/head of family/ warrior. Although his appreciation of insightful, skilled, hardworking women is evident, he had not yet turned his attention to the matrix of empowerment issues facing black women. Black feminists, many of whom have been inspired by Mal-

1963 (Adger W. Cowans/Black Images)

colm's work, have appropriated and transformed the ideas he taught for community empowerment, particularly black cultural and political education, and put them to use.

Malcolm's cultural conservatism on what are now termed "family values" has been echoed by black leaders, like Jesse Jackson, who have had to face "the feminization of poverty"— the spiraling poverty accompanying rising birthrates among teenagers, the widespread unemployment and incarceration of young men, and the devastating erosion of black family life from new epidemics such as crack, AIDS, and widespread homelessness. Nearly thirty years after Malcolm's death, community-based support for the black family is on the agenda.

Malcolm X is teaching you the truth about your own kind. Teaching you the truth about your own culture and about your own past. Restoring your dignity, your human dignity. . . . Making you a man for the first time in four hundred years and the white man doesn't want me to make you a man, he wants you to remain a boy, he wants you to remain a lackey, he wants you to remain dependent on him. . . . No, you teach yourself and stand up for yourself, and respect yourself, and know yourself, and defend yourself, and be yourself.—Malcolm X, from The Wisdom of Malcolm X, *EF Records*

Malcolm X is one of the fathers of African-American studies in America. He popularized the notion of a systematic study of our own civilization and societies throughout the African diaspora. As an avid student of African cultures and history, Malcolm X engaged people in the idea of learning about our past. He spread the word about black scholars then unknown to us, like J. A. Rogers, John Henrik Clarke, Sheikh Anta Diop, and others. He also quoted white historians on African civilization and on slavery, but it was then that the idea of the hidden history of our people, the untaught or censored history, began to take hold. Debates that persist today about "politically correct" history in the academy really have their roots in the exposure of young scholars to Malcolm in the 1960s. Today, many of these young people are professors teaching in black or African studies departments.

"WHITE DEVILS" AND SELF-IMAGE

Malcolm is infamous for calling Caucasians "white devils," a commonly used term in the Honorable Elijah Muhammad's standard speeches. Among its targets, I suppose it ranked below the popular Mr. Charlie (used famously by James

Baldwin), or the widespread late-1960s term "honkie." The most complimentary of the names was probably "The Man," which Malcolm also used. I mention these terms specifically because they have stuck. While they are certainly unlikable, and they no longer have much power to shock, they objectified the anonymous racist individual and pointed to a racist way of thinking among groups and institutions. The words translated as "dominant white patriarchy" and "power structure." To the extent that individual whites bought into the racism of the society and its structures, they were "white devils." Racism is devilish.

Even when Malcolm made us laugh guiltily at his comparisons of black and white physical features and characteristics (material comics today would not "blanch" at using), the message was very clear: the system has made us hate our looks and long for the looks of the "other." When he talked about "that blue-eyed thing" he opened up a Pandora's box of self-loathing on public streets in black communities where we hardly had a language for articulating this desire for physical assimilation. (Books such as Toni Morrison's *The Bluest Eye* would explore this a few years later.)

When Malcolm invoked the image of "that ole pale thing" he made a crude denigration of the dominant culture that was both frightening and cathartic. But it was not a statement about white people—it was a statement about our own mental condition. Malcolm was talking about an intellectual and psychic transformation that had taken place in us since coming here as Africans that parallels some of the skin peels and blue contact lenses that we see around today.

Malcolm pointed out that we had never been at liberty to judge the other by our standards. No one expected whites to understand Malcolm's tactics; white Americans have never been subjected to this kind of rejection of their immutable, biological selves. The issues are still there, and without any Malcolms to pull our coats, the African-American has become, as we hear in the film *Paris Is Burning*, "the most behavior-modified creature in the history of the planet." Malcolm's bottom line was consistent: do not be crippled by your own mind; accept your beauty, your right to life, and act.

By May 1964, after leaving the Nation of Islam, making a pilgrimage to Mecca, and meeting with people in African countries, Malcolm had let go of separatism, and he was saying we should stay where we are and fight for what is ours. And his terms became even more clear:

It doesn't mean that we're anti-white, but it does mean we're anti-exploitation, we're anti-degradation, we're anti-oppression. And if the white man doesn't want us to be anti-him, let him stop oppressing and exploiting and degrading us.—"The Ballot or the Bullet"

HUMAN RIGHTS, NOT CIVIL RIGHTS

We need to expand the civil-rights struggle to a higher level—to the level of human rights. Whenever you are in a civil-rights struggle, whether you know it or not, you are confining yourself to the jurisdiction of Uncle Sam. No one from the outside world can speak out in your behalf as long as your struggle is a civil-rights struggle. . . . Civil rights means you're asking Uncle Sam to treat you right. Human rights are something you were born with. Human rights are your God-given rights. Human rights are the rights that are recognized by all nations of this earth. —"The Ballot or the Bullet"

With the human-rights struggle capturing our attention from all over the world, it still seems that Malcolm was doing some original thinking back in 1964 when he proposed that we take our struggle before the U.N. or World Court. Actually, in 1919 W. E. B. Du Bois proposed that people of color take their grievances before the League of Nations (precursor to the U.N.), particularly the then-colonized people of the African continent. Malcolm is part of a continuum in black thought in America and in the diaspora that has been developing since the nineteenth century.

Today we take causes such as the struggle in South Africa before the court of world opinion. And large numbers of African-Americans have begun supporting such struggles through education, demonstrations, donations, and legislation. In looking at America's intervention in the Third World, Malcolm anticipated the Vietnam anti-war movement, and progressive reaction to U.S. foreign policy ever since.

These ideas of Malcolm's last years actually showed us a direction in which we would have to move: understanding interdependence on the global level. Today we speak of mutual "survival" because we find ourselves living on an endangered planet, but the roots of our action for planetary survival date from ideas articulated in the 1960s, and Malcolm was one of the voices for political interdependence.

Malcolm X represents many different political choices for many people in part because the changes in his thinking happened so quickly. Were it not for the constant presence of

1964 (AP/Wide World)

reporters and electronic media around him we might not have been aware of the slight turns and changes as they came about. In hindsight, these fine points of change in his discourse with his public have become tantalizing clues and signs of where we *think* he may have been going. Some of the theories are bound to be wrong. And some of Malcolm's popularity seems totally divorced from anything Malcolm himself tried to lay down.

Recently I heard a black comedian and movie star say on a talk show that he saw no point in voting because a small group of men were running everything and, in so many words, there is nothing we can do. He said that he preferred to pray and to concentrate on being an artist. The black talk show host asked him wasn't this rather like saying that he wasn't running the plantation so he should just keep singing and keep working—maybe one should add some *action* to one's prayers? The star said he didn't see it doing any good but ended the discussion by saying that he thought Malcolm X and Martin Luther King, Jr., were two of the greatest men who'd ever lived. Malcolm had a great sense of humor and he might have laughed at the scenario, but it does point to the danger of the commercialization of our heroes. If those two men stood for anything it was for a little action with your prayers. A face without an idea is just another costume, another cap or T-shirt, a fad. Use the mind under that cap and check Brother Malcolm out:

The only progress we have made is as consumers. We still don't manufacture anything, we still don't legislate for ourselves. Our politics is still controlled by white people, our economy is still controlled by white people, therefore we have no real say about our future.—The End of White World Supremacy, Four Speeches by Malcolm X *(1970)*

Malcolm X has always represented for me the idea that African-Americans have choices, *that we must make choices,* and that we must bring to our lives our own power to make change. I think of his speeches and ideas in terms of the old story that if you draw a circle in the sand around a scorpion, it will die. Racism, as Malcolm made me understand it, is just such a circle. If we believe this circle of sand is a seamless trap, we will die. As human beings, we can conceive of the circle for what it is, grains of sand, or as a brick wall, a system of man-made devices, or simply as an idea meant to entrap us. We moved as we liked before the circle was drawn. As human beings, we can conceive of ourselves moving outside of it. We can move, even now.

Power in defense of freedom is greater than power in behalf of tyranny and oppression, because power, real power, comes from conviction which produces action, uncompromising action.
—Malcolm X, "Prospects for Freedom in 1965"

1964 (John Launois/Black Star)

ABOUT THE PHOTOGRAPHS

Malcolm's own life is testimony to the fact that the African-American experience is largely undocumented; our history is still part of the hidden history of the country. In this collection are offered the views, close up and in large throngs, taken by men and women, mostly journalists, who had the task of documenting a moment. Printed records do not exist to correspond to all of the events that were photographed, even those regarded as newsworthy at the time.

Malcolm X the public man was photographed most during the last five years of his life. When he was photographed he liked to control the situation of the shoot and he wanted to create certain images for the press. He had several family shots taken to show a softer side of himself because he was acutely aware of being labeled controversial and of newspapers' use of harsh photos that enhanced the fiery, even frightening image. He had photos taken to dispute "disinformation" given out about himself and American Muslims. He knew a photo op before the term came up.

Malcolm was fond of taking photos himself, and Gordon Parks observed that for Malcolm photography was a way of "collecting evidence." In this book are collected more than one hundred photographs of Malcolm X given as "evidence" of how he came into our view.— T. D.

MALCOLM X

The Great Photographs

Malcolm Little, age fourteen.
(Courtesy Betty Shabazz)

"**H**e used to belong to a group which my cousin belonged to that I think was called the Black Panthers. It was a baseball team. They used to play down at [Boston's] Columbus ballpark. I was a kid. I remember him coming by the house. He was just a big, red 'riney' dude who was tight with my cousin. And then later on he became X."
—*William Strickland*

Malcolm Little was born on May 19, 1925, in Omaha, Nebraska, to Louise Norton Little, originally of Grenada, and Earl Little, a Baptist preacher born in Georgia. In the 1920s the Littles were organizers for the nationalist movement led by Marcus Garvey. After Earl Little's death in 1931, Malcolm's family was separated by serious crises and Malcolm was sent to several foster homes. At fifteen, he went to live with his sister Ella in Boston, where he worked odd jobs and was attracted to life in the "fast lane." Work on the railroad brought him to Harlem and within a couple of years Malcolm moved to New York.

Facing page: Malcolm Little, age eighteen, at the time of a 1944 Boston arrest for larceny that resulted in a three-month suspended sentence.
(Photographer unknown)

Having come of age in the streets of Boston and New York, at age twenty Malcolm Little was imprisoned for larceny and breaking and entering. A program of self-education reawakened the racial consciousness shared by his activist parents and he was converted to the teachings of the Honorable Elijah Muhammad. On his release in 1952, he was granted the Nation of Islam's "X" surname and became known as Malcolm X.

Malcolm X became minister of the Nation of Islam's New York Temple No. 7 in 1954. A year earlier, the FBI, hot on the trail of possible communists, had opened a file on Malcolm while he was still in jail, owing to a line written in a personal letter. He was a subject of continuous investigation until his death.

The Black Muslims, as the Nation of Islam soon was known, came to the attention of the Ameri-can public around 1959. In the early 1960s, Malcolm X became the group's most prominent and visible spokesman. Membership had been estimated at about six thousand when Malcolm began his ministry; by 1959 it reached more than 100,000. Malcolm's eloquence, incisiveness, and wit brought him a growing following among young non-Muslim African-Americans.

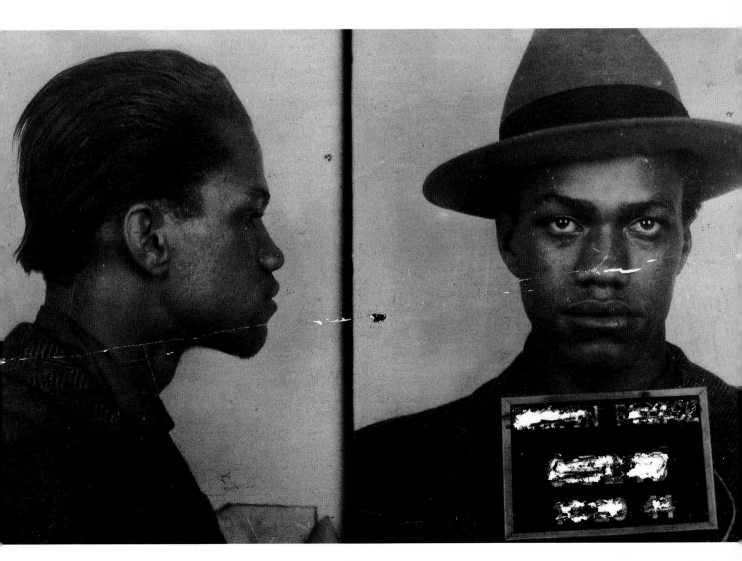

American Committee on Africa
rally in Harlem honoring a visit
by Kwame Nkrumah, leader of
newly independent Ghana, 1960.
Seated directly behind Malcolm,
waving: Congressman Adam
Clayton Powell, Jr., and
Nkrumah; to left of Malcolm,
ACOA chairman Chuck Stone.

Between June and October of
1960 independence was won in
the African countries now known
as Benin, Burkina Faso, Chad,
Congo, Gabon, Ivory Coast, Mali,
Senegal, Somalia, and Zaire.
(New York Age, Collection Chuck Stone)

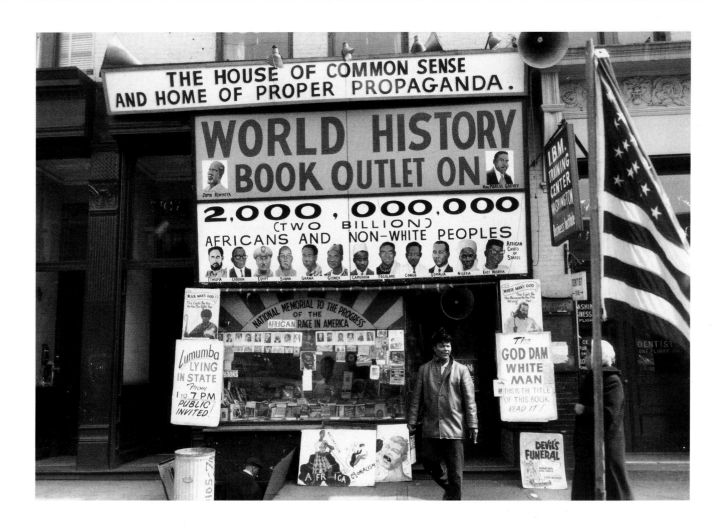

*N*ational Memorial African
Bookstore, run by Lewis Micheaux,
located at 125th Street and
Seventh Avenue, New York,
1961. Sign stating [Patrice]
"Lumumba is lying in state" refers
to an effigy of the recently assassinated Congolese prime minister
then on display inside the store.
(Henri Cartier-Bresson/Magnum)

*Malcolm speaking outside
Micheaux's National Memorial
African Bookstore, 125th Street,
Harlem, 1960. (Robert L. Haggins)*

In Malcolm's early days in Harlem
he conducted what he called "fish-
ing expeditions" (for possible converts) at open rallies on 125th
Street. Photographer Robert L.
Haggins recalls a time when he
spoke from a stepladder and hardly
anyone appeared at the temple.
He would end his speeches by saying, "Thank you for listening,
and may we meet again in the
light of understanding."

"I first saw Malcolm at Micheaux's. He would come in there, and he and Micheaux would talk. Micheaux was, of course, very well known then throughout Harlem as a major nationalist spokesman himself, and he would speak out on the street corner. Sometimes he would have Malcolm speak right there in front of the store. He would introduce Malcolm at a rally. The more I listened, the more their broad analysis in terms of our lack of power, our people having no sense of their history, all those basic nationalist tenets— internal self-contempt, lack of ability to cooperate—began to resonate."—James Turner

(Robert L. Haggins)

During a two-year period, 1959 to 1961, Malcolm X took photographer Eve Arnold to an array of Muslim-owned businesses—stores, restaurants, bakeries, and tailor shops—set up to help achieve economic independence for the African-American community.

The development of restaurants and other food businesses was encouraged by the Nation of Islam because the dietary restrictions of the religion discouraged use of too many processed foods and excluded pork and a number of other staples of the traditional southern black diet. Use of tobacco, caffeine, alcohol, and other stimulants was also prohibited.

Arnold recalls that Malcolm tried to set up every shot she was to take. It took her two years of photographing him to get him to agree to a portrait session (pages 12 and 48–49). C. Eric Lincoln's The Black Muslims in America had just come out and the Nation of Islam was becoming nationally known, but Life magazine, which originally planned to publish Arnold's article, opted not to run the photographs (Esquire published them in 1963).

Muslim restaurant, circa February 1961.

(Henri Cartier-Bresson/Magnum)

Chicago, 1967. Muhammad
Speaks, *the national newspaper
of the Nation of Islam, was
founded a decade earlier,
in 1957, by Malcolm X.*
(Robert A. Sengstacke)

"**T**hey had this whole process by
which they would sell the paper.
Muslims had to buy the papers
first and then you had to go out
and sell them to recoup your dough.
But it was a wonderful mechanism
for consolidating true believers, because you had to go out there and
expound on your faith, face the
ridicule and the scorn. And you
had to sell, because if you didn't
sell, you were in trouble."—
William Strickland

Facing page, both: Chicago, 1961.
(Eve Arnold/Magnum)

Nation of Islam convention,
Uline Arena, Washington, D.C.,
June 25, 1961. (Eve Arnold/Magnum)

Facing page: The Honorable Elijah
Muhammad, prophet and leader of
the Nation of Islam, at the 369th
Regiment Armory, 142nd Street
and Fifth Avenue, New York,
August 27, 1961.
(Eve Arnold/Magnum)

Malcolm *became a popular Mus-*
lim leader, and as one of Muham-
mad's most resourceful organizers,
he was assigned to establish temples
(later termed "mosques" by
Malcolm) in numerous cities.

"**I** *listened to James Lawson, Carlos*
Cook, and other famed street-
corner preachers, and that began
a budding consciousness. But then
Malcolm broke on the scene. He
was the most dramatic speaker.
What I found impressive about
Malcolm was not just his eloquent
command of words but his ability
to reason very complex ideas in a
way that was accessible to people
who were not intellectuals. I heard
Malcolm speaking on the few occa-
sions that Elijah Muhammad
came to New York. He would 'open
up' for him. We'd all go to hear
Malcolm."—James Turner

George Lincoln Rockwell and members of his American Nazi party attended the Nation of Islam convention in June 1961 to discuss a partition of America. According to photographer Arnold, after several hours it was announced that Elijah Muhammad was ill, and Malcolm X presided. Later, in January 1965, Malcolm made public a telegram he sent Rockwell saying, "I am no longer held in check from fighting white suprem-acists by Elijah Muhammad's separatist Black Muslim movement," and warning "that if your present racist agitation against our people there in Alabama causes physical harm to Reverend King or any other black American, that you and your Ku Klux Klan friends will be met with maximum physical retaliation from those of us who . . . believe in asserting our right of self-defense—by any means necessary."

Facing page, both: Uline Arena, Washington, D.C., June 25, 1961.
(Eve Arnold/Magnum)

369th Regiment Armory,
Harlem, August 27, 1961.
(Eve Arnold/Magnum)

"**M**alcolm was clearly established
as the reason blacks were being
attracted to the Nation of Islam.
It wasn't because of Elijah
Muhammad. Malcolm was the
charismatic personality, the driv-
ing force. But he was always very
careful to pay homage or defer to
Elijah Muhammad. Malcolm
was very cautious and careful."
—Chuck Stone

Pages 48 and 49: 1961
(Eve Arnold/Magnum)

International Amphitheatre,
Chicago, 1962. (Eve Arnold/Magnum)

Malcolm X, Community Church,
East 35th Street, New York City,
1962. (Bob Adelman)

Between 1960 and 1962,
Malcolm participated in a number
of public discussions with Bayard
Rustin—a key strategist for
Martin Luther King, Jr., and
until 1963 executive secretary
of the War Resisters League—
on the subject of separation versus
integration. The first of these
was recorded in 1960 in the
studios of the New York radio
station *WBAI*; Malcolm was on
the defensive and Rustin had
the upper hand. In January
1962, the War Resisters League
sponsored a debate at a New
York City church. More than a
thousand people attended, and
eyewitnesses say Malcolm clearly
won. A later debate, at Howard
University, was organized by
students Stokely Carmichael and
Cleveland Sellers, who became
activists with the Student
Nonviolent Coordinating
Committee (SNCC).

*Bayard Rustin, Community
Church, East 35th Street, New
York City, 1962. (Bob Adelman)*

*Pages 52 and 53: 125th Street and
Seventh Avenue, Harlem, 1962.
(Klytus Smith/Black Images)*

"**I** *was at the* New York Age *office,
a storefront on 125th Street, one
day and Malcolm came in to buy
an ad. He was one of those people
in Harlem that you knew. The
Muslims were gaining strength
in those days. He was very soft-
spoken when he was one-on-one,
very gentlemanly. The ad cost over
$100, and I was startled as he sat
there and counted out the money
in one-dollar bills."—Louise Stone*

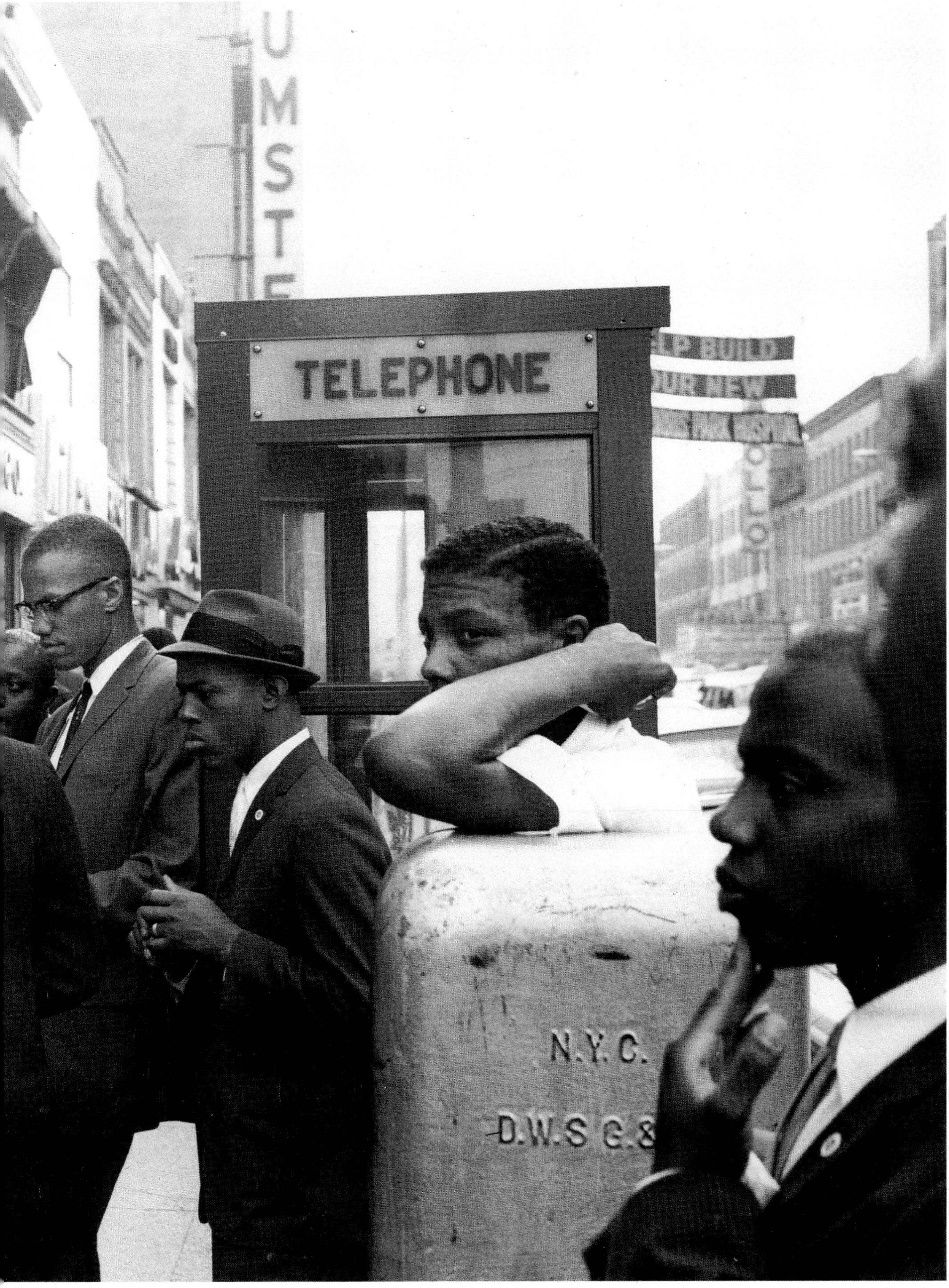
TELEPHONE
N.Y.C.

Protest at New York City Criminal Court, with aides Minister Benjamin Karim and Minister James Shabazz, January 11, 1963. (Robert L. Haggins)

Malcolm X became well known during this period for addressing the issue of police brutality against African-Americans and leading protests over incidents involving police and Muslims, including a police assault on a Rochester, New York, mosque in which Muslims were arrested.

On December 25, 1962, two Muslims were arrested while selling Muhammad Speaks *in Times Square. They were charged with disorderly conduct; police said the Muslims had blocked the subway, bumped into a woman, and assaulted them. Hundreds of Muslims protested at the courts in January and February.*

*Outside New York City
Criminal Court building,
1963.* (Robert L. Haggins)

57

Outside New York City Criminal
Court building, 1963.
(Robert L. Haggins)

*Outside New York City Criminal
Court building, 1963.*
(Gordon Parks)

*Outside New York City Criminal
Court building, 1963.*
(Robert L. Haggins)

*Malcolm with fliers, New York
City Criminal Court building,
1963. (Gordon Parks)*

Before a shocked courtroom, the
two Muslims were convicted. On
February 1, 1963, one received
sixty days and one was given a
suspended sentence. The protesters
marched solemnly from the courts
to Times Square.

*Pages 62 and 63: Courtroom,
1963. (Gordon Parks)*

*Pages 64 and 65: Times Square,
1963. (Bob Adelman/Magnum)*

*Rally, the Honorable Elijah
Muhammad speaking, with the
Fruit of Islam guard, Chicago,
1967. (AP/Wide World)*

"**T**heir social line and their political analysis was on time and on
point. It had a salutary effect on
the community. I had never seen
us together like that. But it was
essentially an autocratic organization. Most brothers and sisters
of my time, we were not into the
religious thing, because we had
become alienated from the religious
opiate—we liked the communal
relation, the cultural side. And the
Nation had a fighting spirit."—
James Turner

Chicago, 1963. (Gordon Parks)

The Muslim women's corps was led by Elijah Muhammad's daughter Ethel Sharrieff (foreground) at the Chicago headquarters temple. Muslim women dressed in modest clothing covering most of the body and were trained (in women-only classes) in traditional homemaking arts, reading, mathematics, and religion. In the temple, women, dressed in white, were seated separately from men. Singing and dancing, historically emphasized in depictions of blacks, were prohibited.

Pages 68 and 69: *Temple No. 7 restaurant, 1963.* (Gordon Parks)

The Temple No. 7 restaurant, at 116th Street and Lenox Avenue in Harlem, was a busy meeting place for temple members and a second office for Malcolm X. He often asked people requesting meetings and interviews to meet him there, providing many with their first opportunity to visit a Harlem institution and to have their first taste of the "bean pie" made famous by the Nation of Islam. Temple No. 7 restaurant also became popular with non-Muslims looking for a good, inexpensive meal and a comfortable place to meet in a neighborhood being ravaged by the urban decline of the 1960s.

Husbandry
MAN = Husband = Father
MAN = Protector = Provider
MAN = Controller = Elevator
MAN = Authority = Head
GOD GOD

Both: University of Islam, Chicago, 1963. (Gordon Parks)

Life for members of the Nation of Islam was structured by instruction in the male and female roles in family life and a strict moral code of behavior. The University of Islam in Chicago educated members in basic subjects as well as in Islam, and granted high school diplomas. The daily regimen included prayer six times daily— facing east at sunrise and sunset. Muslim theology dismissed the idea of a reward in the hereafter, preferring a reward in life.

"When you walked into the mosque they used to have this blackboard. The blackboard was divided into Christianity and Islam. And Malcolm would talk that stuff about how when the white man came to Africa you had the land, and he had the Bible, and when he left, he had the land, and you had the Bible."—William Strickland

Children's class, University of
Islam, Chicago, 1963. *(Gordon Parks)*

Facing page: Father and son, both
Muslims, pray in their Brooklyn,
New York, home, 1963.
(Gordon Parks)

"**W**hat I liked most about the
Nation was the ambience inside.
Here was a small place that had a
certain kind of tranquillity, a zone
that was different than all the rest
of Harlem. People walked in and
they got transformed. They were
respectful of each other. When people came in there, their behavior
changed. Lenox Avenue and 116th
was one of the roughest sections of
Harlem, but none of that went
down in front of the mosque."—
James Turner

Rally in Harlem, Seventh Avenue between 125th and 126th streets, early 1963. Dick Gregory at microphone; Malcolm X and former Manhattan borough president Hulan Jack, seated; photographer Gordon Parks in background.
(O'Neal L. Abel)

Rally in Harlem, Seventh Avenue between 125th and 126th streets, early 1963. Malcolm X with lawyer Percy Sutton (then president of the New York branch of the NAACP), left, and Hulan Jack, right. (O'Neal L. Abel)

Rally in Harlem, Seventh Avenue between 125th and 126th streets, early 1963. Congressman Adam Clayton Powell, Jr., left of Malcolm X, and Hulan Jack, on right. (Gordon Parks)

Malcolm is most often remembered by those who saw him as a leader "teaching" on the street corners of Harlem before thousands of listeners. As he cited books and newspapers, which he held up from a pile he often carried with him, he gave talks covering an array of subjects spiced with down-home wit and inventive improvisations in response to the crowd.

Facing page: Rally in Harlem, Seventh Avenue and 125th Street, early 1963. (Gordon Parks)

VICTIMS PAY $90,000 FOR "JUSTICE"
25c
EXTRA
25c
Muslim Story of:
SEVEN UNARMED NEGROES
IN COLD BLOOD BY
ANGELES POLICE

The headline SEVEN UNARMED NEGROES SHOT IN COLD BLOOD refers to a Los Angeles police and Muslim conflict on the night of April 27, 1962, that ended in the shooting death of Nation of Islam member Ronald Stokes. A melee began when policemen stopped to check out two men who were selling clothing on the street. The ensuing hostilities quickly turned into a near riot. Early reports said seventy-five officers were involved, along with police cars from three divisions and many Muslim men. It ended with police shooting seven Muslims, wounding six, and killing Stokes.

Malcolm was dispatched to Los Angeles by Elijah Muhammad immediately following the incident and again, one year later, in April 1963, when the case was brought before a jury. Fourteen Muslims were arrested; one was charged with assault with intent to kill and the others with assault and interference with police officers.

During the fifty-one-day trial, spectators were barred from the courtroom and the building was ringed by three hundred police officers. It was reported in court that the incident involved nine officers and a "score" of Muslims, that two Muslims were "seriously injured" besides Stokes, and several policemen were badly hurt. According to the newspaper Muhammad Speaks, one officer who shot at the Muslims admitted that he knew Stokes had no weapon when he was shot, and ballistics testimony showed that the wounded cop was shot by his own partner; the gun was found in a sewer.

Los Angeles, 1963. (Gordon Parks)

Los Angeles, 1963. (Gordon Parks)

"I remember the night Malcolm spoke after this brother Stokes was killed in Los Angeles, and he was holding up a huge photo showing the autopsy with a bullet hole at the back of the head. He was angry then, he was dead angry. It was a huge rally. But he was never out of control. The press tried to project his militancy as wild, unthought-ful, and out of control. But Malcolm was always controlled, always thinking what to do in political terms."—James Turner

Facing page, both: Los Angeles courtroom, April–May 1963. Malcolm X displaying pictures of Muslim Ronald Stokes, killed by police a year earlier. (Gordon Parks)

Facing page and above: 1963.
(Gordon Parks)

Malcolm's anger alarmed many in Los Angeles, though, because there were Muslims who wanted to take their vengeance out on the killers. According to Malcolm's close aide, Minister Benjamin Karim, a Los Angeles police department official called Elijah Muhammad and asked him to send Malcolm back to New York.

While the trial was still in progress, Malcolm and photographer Gordon Parks flew to Phoenix, Arizona, to see Elijah Muhammad, who told them, "Every one of the Muslims should have died before they allowed an aggressor to come into their mosque. They were fearless, but they didn't trust Allah completely."

At the close of the trial in Los Angeles eleven of the fourteen Black Muslims tried were convicted.

By May 1963, there were signs
that relations between Malcolm
and the rest of the Nation of Islam
leadership were strained. Before
Gordon Parks's May 31, 1963,
Life *magazine article went to
press, his editors asked for a portrait of the Muslim leadership.
When Parks was arranging the
Phoenix photo session, he asked
Herbert Muhammad if he should
have Malcolm X fly out with him.
Herbert Muhammad said that
was not necessary. When Parks
said that* Life *magazine was interested in all the Muslim leaders,
Muhammad repeated that it would
not be necessary for Malcolm to
be there.*

*Nation of Islam leadership,
Phoenix, Arizona, May 1963:
the Honorable Elijah Muhammad
(center) and his wife, Clara; (back
row, left to right) son Elijah, Jr.;
son-in-law Raymond Sharrieff,
head of the Fruit of Islam; grand-
son Hasan Sharrieff; and son
Herbert. (Gordon Parks)*

116th Street and Lenox Avenue, Harlem, 1963. Malcolm leaves the Temple No. 7 restaurant to go to speak at 115th and Lenox. Encircling Malcolm in bottom left photograph are (clockwise from left) Minister James Shabazz (with glasses and hat); a minister from Buffalo, New York; Minister Louis X (now Farrakhan); Minister Benjamin Karim (with sunglasses); Brother Gladstone; Minister Henry (facing Malcolm); and Captain Joseph (in light jacket). By 1963, his weekly talks in the summer drew thousands of listeners, and the police were forced to cordon off the streets.
(All, Robert L. Haggins)

"I had just moved to Harlem. It was the first night I was there, and I went for a walk and there was a rally going on. Of course, I had heard about Malcolm before that, but it was mostly the kind of negative things they were running about him in the press then. I felt as though I was hearing the truth. I had never heard anyone speak with such clarity and forcefulness. And he just stimulated me. I found if he mentioned a book or a magazine article, I would try to find it. You hear people use that cliché about University of the Streets. It really was that."—A. Peter Bailey

1963 *(Robert L. Haggins)*

By the summer of 1963 Malcolm X had become a nationally famous figure, featured in Life magazine and in a lengthy interview by Alex Haley in Playboy. He was the second most sought-after speaker at colleges and universities across the country. (Presidential candidate Barry Goldwater topped the list.)

The protests ongoing in the South now had counterparts in northern cities, where there were weeks-long demonstrations over de facto segregation in schools, housing, and jobs. This meant that northern blacks, the natural constituency of the Nation of Islam, were even more ready to hear activist proposals and for figures like Malcolm to build a northern movement linked to events in the South. Malcolm had already been talking about the failure of simple integration to address endemic racial problems, as evidenced by black life in the North, and now the chronic nature of discrimination was the subject of widespread protest.

At the same time, though, Elijah Muhammad told Malcolm not to help or join any demonstrations sponsored by the civil-rights organizations, including the upcoming March on Washington, which would be the largest demonstration ever held. Malcolm's response was to continue to appear at events taking place and to keep up with his weekly rallies in Harlem.

Malcolm X had a reputation for drawing the largest crowds at Harlem rallies. The press came out for the rally on June 29, 1963, because Malcolm had invited many members of the black leadership to come and talk.

"We invited Dr. Adam Clayton Powell, Dr. Roy Wilkins, Dr. Whitney Young, Dr. James Farmer, Dr. Edward Davis, the right Reverend Martin Luther King, Dr. Gardner C. Taylor, Dr. Ralph Bunche, Dr. A. Phillip Randolph, Professor James Martin, and Dr. James Forman.

"We invited all these doctors to come out, and since they are doctors, give their analysis, their diagnosis of the ailments that our people are afflicted with here in America. Then we wanted them to offer their solution." None of them appeared, and Malcolm simply gave his analysis.

115th Street and Lenox Avenue, Harlem, June 29, 1963.
(Ted Russell)

June 29, 1963.
(Bob Adelman/Magnum)

"It wasn't just one Saturday. He did the rallies for about four or five Saturdays in the summer. It was a learning experience in every sense of the word. Those of us who worked with Brother Malcolm don't try to make claims that what he was doing nobody had ever done before. He was a continuation going back to Martin Delaney [1812–85; journalist and Reconstruction political figure interested in maintaining African-American ties to Africa]. He made those connections.

"He very much wanted the Africans to connect the movement in this country with the movement against colonialism. He was talking about it in his speeches early. Like Lumumba, he was the one saying that Lumumba had been killed by the American government, and of course everybody denied it. He knew about these people because he followed what was happening in Africa in terms of the anticolonialist movement."
—A. Peter Bailey

June 29, 1963.
(*Bob Adelman/Magnum*)

"**M**alcolm made it plain, in the terminology, when he started talking about history from slavery to the present. He used to read from a book that's hard to find now, a book called Anti-Slavery [Origins of the Civil War], *by Dwight Lowell Dumond, a white historian. And Malcolm would quote from the dude and he'd say, 'Now, you know this is true, 'cause the white man said it.' So as Malcolm took you through the history from Africa through slavery and hooked it up to the present, you gained the sense that the form may change, the faces may change, the actors may change, but the fundamental relationship to you hadn't changed.*"
—William Strickland

June 29, 1963.
(Bob Adelman/Magnum)

Brooklyn demonstration jointly sponsored by Brooklyn CORE, the NAACP, the Urban League, and the Bedford-Stuyvesant Ministerial Conference, July 1963. People demonstrated for more than three weeks at the site of the Downstate Medical Center, under construction across from the Kings County Hospital. The action started July 10, after groups had pleaded for an end to discrimination on the job site. By July 30, police had arrested 603 sit-ins.

Both, Brooklyn, New York, July/August 1963.
(Bob Adelman/Magnum)

*Malcolm X at the opening of a
New York travel agency run by
Muslims, 1963.* (Robert L. Haggins)

Photographer Robert L. Haggins
remembers accompanying Malcolm X to the United Nations in
the summer of 1963 as Malcolm
went on a mission to dispel charges
that Muslims abroad did not rec-
ognize American Muslims. He
met with and had pictures taken
with Muslim diplomats from
West Africa.

"**M**alcolm felt it was very important
for Africans to start thinking of the
movement here as part of a world-
wide movement against colonialism
and European domination. He
kept up with what was going on
over there. He was invited to the
U.N. a lot, to affairs and recep-
tions, by African diplomats that
he got to know."—A. Peter Bailey

*At the United Nations, summer
1963. (Robert L. Haggins)*

Prior to the February 26, 1964, Sonny Liston-Cassius Clay prize-fight, Elijah Muhammad had told Malcolm X not to be seen as close to Clay because he thought the young boxer would lose the Liston fight and possibly embarrass the Nation of Islam. Malcolm had also been ordered to refrain from public

Malcolm X with his family. Facing page, at home in East Elmhurst, Queens, with daughters Qubilah (left) and Attallah, 1963. Above, with Cassius Clay at the fighter's Miami training camp, with (left to right) wife Betty and daughters Attallah, Qubilah, Ilyasah, 1963–1964. (Both, Robert L. Haggins)

statements for ninety days following a furor caused by remarks he made in November after the assassination of President John F. Kennedy. Elijah Muhammad and Malcolm X were still not on good terms, but Clay and Malcolm were friends. Malcolm went to visit Clay unofficially and was there when Clay surprised many by winning the title.

"I used to see him when I went down to Florida to see Adam Powell. He would be down there sitting in this black hotel. He and Clay would always sit at the counter in the luncheonette. I'd seen him there two or three times. At the time I didn't know what he was doing. It never occurred to me that Clay was converting."—Chuck Stone

Pages 104–107: Malcolm X and Cassius Clay in a Miami restaurant after Clay won the heavyweight championship from Sonny Liston, February 26, 1964.
(All, Bob Gomel)

After the fight, Clay, who had quietly joined the Nation of Islam in 1961, publicly announced that he was a Muslim and his name thereafter would be Muhammad Ali.

Shortly after the fight, Malcolm was back in Harlem and photographer Robert L. Haggins went to a room Malcolm had at the Hotel Theresa, where Malcolm was sitting on the bed. From nowhere a fist came at him. It was Muhammad Ali, teasing him. As a Muslim, Ali was under a directive from Elijah Muhammad not to talk with Malcolm X and soon would distance himself from his mentor. Malcolm's split from the Nation of Islam was then only days away.

Muhammad Ali walks in Harlem with Malcolm X as fans congratulate the new champ, February 1964. (Robert L. Haggins)

*Malcolm X at the time of his break
with the Nation of Islam. New
York City, March 10, 1964.*
(*Truman Moore*)

On March 8, 1964, the New York Times *ran a story stating that Malcolm X was leaving the Black Muslims.*

That same day, the Nation of Islam sent a letter to Malcolm asking him to vacate his home, which was owned by the organization. In another interview that day he said that he felt the Nation could "not afford" to let him live because of his knowledge of the group's inner workings.

On March 10, 1964, Malcolm was taken to lunch by the editors of Life *magazine and photographer Truman Moore documented the meeting.*

New York City, March 10, 1964.
(Truman Moore)

New York City, March 10, 1964.
(Truman Moore)

Pages 114 and 115: Press confer-
ence, Park-Sheraton Hotel, New
York City, March 12, 1964.
(AP/Wide World)

Press conference, National Memorial African Bookstore, Harlem, March 12, 1964.

(UPI/Bettmann)

On March 12, 1964, Malcolm held a series of press conferences announcing the formation of Muslim Mosque, Inc. (MMI), a Muslim group with a black nationalist social program. At this time Malcolm intended to continue Muslim practices while emphasizing political action in MMI. Referring to himself as Brother Malcolm, he predicted that 1964 would be the "bloodiest year yet in the civil-rights fight."

First speech after break with the
Nation of Islam, Rockland Palace,
155th Street and Eighth Avenue,
Harlem, March 23, 1964.
(Truman Moore)

Rockland Palace, March 23, 1964.
(Truman Moore)

Malcolm's departure from the Nation caused enormous interest throughout the African-American community and with the press. Many who were interested in him but not in joining Elijah Muhammad's organization looked to see if a more secular organization would emerge, which might allow larger numbers of blacks to take part. Journalists wanted to know if he would renounce separatism and espousal of the doctrine that labeled whites "devils." The break exposed him to a crushing barrage of public questioning.

Rockland Palace, March 23, 1964.
(Truman Moore)

Rockland Palace, March 23, 1964.
(*Truman Moore*)

Malcolm X and the Rev. Martin Luther King, Jr., had their only meeting, by chance, on Capitol Hill, March 26, 1964. According to his biographers, King was on the Hill to discuss strategy with several Democratic senators.
(AP/World Wide)

Malcolm X and Adam Clayton Powell, Jr., 1964, at a meeting (above) to show support for a black boycott of New York City schools in protest of their "de facto" segregation. Powell also invited Malcolm to come speak to his congregation

at the Abyssinian Baptist Church. The newly independent Brother Malcolm quickly moved to make more visible a dialogue with a wide spectrum of political activists, American and African.
(Dr. Laurance G. Henry Collection)

In 1964 Malcolm X made two lengthy trips to the Middle East and Africa. In April and May he traveled to Cairo and Alexandria in Egypt, Jedda and Mecca in Saudi Arabia, and to Beirut, Nigeria, Ghana, Liberia, Senegal, Morocco, and Algeria, where he celebrated his thirty-ninth birthday.

The trip to Mecca was a time of life-changing introspection, as he wrote about it, in which he realized a larger vision of human potential. He later described a moment of transcendence in which all humanity was one, an undivided assembly of human beings before God. He said then that "on this pilgrimage, what I have seen and experienced has forced me to rearrange much of my thought patterns previously held and to toss aside some of my previous conclusions."

Malcolm became interested in moving toward orthodox Islam as practiced throughout the world. His trip to Mecca and talks with Muslims overseas had made him realize how much the Nation of Islam had altered traditional Islamic ideas.

In Saudi Arabia Malcolm was the guest of Prince Faisal, and in Ghana he spoke before the parliament and met with President Nkrumah, whom he'd met in Harlem in 1960. In Ghana he met young black Americans who had left the States to live in Africa, among them writers Julian Mayfield and Maya Angelou and the painter Tom Feelings. In Nigeria he spoke at the University of Ibadan, and in Monrovia, Liberia, he saw a culture influenced by African-Americans who established a colony there in the nineteenth century. Concerned with Malcolm's meetings with Arabs and public statements he might make about the United States, the U.S. government maintained surveillance on him throughout both trips.

Cairo, September 1964.
(John Launois/Black Star)

*Both: Mosque of Muhammad
Ali, Cairo, September 1964.*

(John Launois/Black Star)

"I have been blessed to visit the Holy
City of Mecca. I have made my
seven circuits around the Ka'ba,
led by a young Mutawaf named
Muhammad. I drank water from
the well of Zem Zem. I ran seven
times back and forth between
the hills of Mount Al-Safa and
Al-Marwah. I have prayed in the
ancient city of Mina, and I have
prayed on Mount Arafat. All
praise is due to Allah, the Lord of
all the Worlds."—Malcolm X

From July 9 to November 24 Malcolm X was on a second journey to Africa. On this trip he saw a great deal more of Africa and its revolutionaries. During the beginning of the "Freedom Summer" in Mississippi, Malcolm was in Addis Ababa, Ethiopia, attending the African Summit Conference, a meeting of leaders from all over the continent. He called on the group to bring the cause of African-Americans to the United Nations. The Organization of African Unity (OAU) released a statement against the brutality then being meted out against civil-rights activists in Mississippi. In Cairo he met Shirley Graham Du Bois, widow of African-American leader W. E. B. Du Bois, conferred with Muslim educators, and in both Alexandria and Addis Ababa spoke to more than six hundred Muslim students.

Egypt, September 1964.
(John Launois/Black Star)

Egypt, September 1964.
(*John Launois/Black Star*)

Leaving a second summit in August, Malcolm traveled to Kenya, where he ran into SNCC activists John Lewis and Donald Harris and spent two days discussing the civil rights movement. He flew from Kenya to Tanzania with President Jomo Kenyatta of Kenya and Ugandan President Milton Obote. He made a return visit to Nigeria and made his last stop in Conakry, French West Africa (now Guinea).

Facing page: Betty Shabazz with daughters while Malcolm was traveling to Africa, 1964. From left, Qubilah, Gamilah (asleep), Betty, Attallah, and Ilyasah. Note map of Africa, showing large sections of former European colonial territories. (John Launois/Black Star)

Below: Malcolm, now publicly referring to himself as El-Hajj Malik El-Shabazz, on return from Mecca, May 1964. To his left is Charles 37X (Kenyatta).
(Robert L. Haggins)

At a press conference after Malcolm returned from Mecca, he was quizzed about the riots that took place in Harlem (as well as in New Jersey, Chicago, and Philadelphia) while he was away, some reporters even insinuating he was in some way responsible. Malcolm took the occasion to condemn U.S. policy in Africa.

Malcolm X in Harlem office with
Lewis Micheaux (right) and
another associate, June 3, 1964.
(Marvin Lichtner)

Cairo, Egypt, meeting with
Sheikh Abdel Rahman Tag (right),
future rector of Al Azhar, the first
Muslim university in the world,
July 18, 1964. (UPI/Bettmann)

*Malcolm X at the Audubon
Ballroom with Sheikh Hassen
from Mecca (in turban) and Abu
Rahman Mohammad Babu, with
whom he met during his travels
in Africa. New York City,
November 29, 1964.*
(Robert L. Haggins)

Malcolm flew to Paris in early February 1965 for a scheduled appearance and was refused entry into the country. He returned to London, where he had addressed the First Congress of the Council of African Organizations and the London School of Economics. During this period he was getting a second organization off the ground, a nonreligious group dedicated to social change called the Organization of Afro-American Unity (modeled after the OAU), and meeting privately with leaders from the traditional civil-rights organizations.

London, February 9, 1965.
(AP/Wide World)

"**T**he black student group I was in wrote him a letter saying we'd heard he'd suspended security provisions [at OAAU meetings]— people weren't being searched fully like before. We told him we thought that was not wise, in fact more security should be in place. He wrote back, and after thanking us, said, 'Brothers, our people are patted down and knocked down every day of their lives. We want them to come in here and know that they are among their brothers and sisters.'"—James Turner

"**H**e called me while he was in Chicago [January 30] and said he just wanted to meet with me. He didn't believe he had long to live. There were six detectives from the state Attorney General's office guarding him. They walked into the hotel. I was in the lobby waiting for him, and I rushed up and they grabbed me. I had to get inside this ring of men around him. When we got up on the floor where he was staying, there was a black guy waiting there with a shotgun, and they chased him and he ran down the back stairs. They chased him and he got away."
—Chuck Stone

London, February 9, 1965.
(Topham/The Image Works)

Malcolm arriving home the day
of the fire bombing of his home
in East Elmhurst, Queens,
February 14, 1965.
(UPI/Bettmann)

"I remember him saying that Sunday, 'The way I feel today, I feel like I shouldn't even be here.' And he looked kind of harried that day. I had never seen him look harried before. And I think it was because the fire bombing was the first time that his children were put in danger, and that puts another whole burden on a man. A man can deal with threats to himself. And I think that was one of the reasons he was looking so harried that Sunday. It puts a whole burden on a man. And he was a human being."—A. Peter Bailey

The last known portrait of Malcolm X, February 18, 1965.
(Robert L. Haggins)

*OAAU meeting, Audubon
Ballroom, Harlem, February 21,
1965, 3:10 P.M. (AP/Wide World)*

As Malcolm X was getting ready
to speak at an OAAU meeting
in the Audubon Ballroom on
February 21, 1965, a scuffle broke
out in the hallway of the second
floor. A number of his security
people left the room to check out
the noise. After Malcolm greeted
the audience, saying, "As Salaam
Alaikum," shots rang out. At least
two men had risen from their seats
with handguns and fired. Another
man shot at close range with a
sawed-off shotgun, and Malcolm
was fatally wounded by gunshots
to the chest. It was 3:10 P.M.

"**M**alcolm had sent me to bring Rev.
Milton Galamison backstage. He
was going to make an appeal for
clothing for Malcolm's family because they had been burned up in
the fire bombing. I had been out
there in the little alcove off the
main room maybe ten or fifteen
minutes when I heard, you know,
the shooting start. I heard him say,
'As Salaam Alaikum' and the next
thing I heard was shots. I ran into
there, heard people screaming, and
jumped onstage, and I saw him
lying on the stage, you know, with
all the holes."—A. Peter Bailey

February 21, 1965.
(AP/Wide World)

In the confusion the gunmen escaped from the hall. One man, Talmadege Hayer (a.k.a. Thomas Hagan), was caught outside by security men who shot him in the leg. Police officers then struggled with Hagan and arrested him. Subsequently Hagan was indicted, along with Norman 3X Butler and Thomas 15X Johnson, for the murder of Malcolm X.

Pages 144 and 145: Malcolm X being taken on a stretcher from the Audubon to Columbia Presbyterian Hospital Center, where he was declared dead on arrival.
(UPI/Bettmann)

*Betty Shabazz (holding coat) out-
side the Audubon, February 21,
1965. Mrs. Shabazz was then
carrying twin daughters Malaak
and Malikah, who were born later
in the year. (AP/Wide World)*

*Facing page, top: Mourners wait
outside the Unity Funeral Chapel,
126th Street and Eighth Avenue,
to pay their respects, February 24,
1965. (AP/Wide World)*

*Facing page, bottom: Demonstra-
tors picket a 125th Street store that
was not, like many others, closed
after a community call for a day of
mourning, February 26, 1965.
(UPI/Bettmann)*

*More than a year after the assassi-
nation, following a two-month
trial, the three accused men were
sentenced to life imprisonment. The
trial raised as many questions as it
answered, and the event is still the
source of inquiry and speculation.*

Elijah Muhammad in his Chicago home, accompanied by his son Herbert Muhammad (left) and minister James Shabazz (right), February 22, 1965. The head of the Nation of Islam said he was shocked by the death of Malcolm X, but "we are not disturbed because we are innocent." At the time many people suspected the Nation of Islam was involved in the assassination, particularly because upon leaving the Nation Malcolm had candidly expressed his conviction that the group would make him a target. *(AP/Wide World)*

An early-morning explosion set the Nation of Islam's mosque no. 7 on fire. New York City, February 23, 1965. (AP/Wide World)

February 24, 1965.
(UPI/Bettmann)

Facing page: February 1965.
(Bob Adelman)

Pages 152 and 153: Funeral service, Faith Temple Church of God in Christ, Harlem, February 27, 1965. Malcolm was buried at Ferncliff Cemetery, Hartsdale, New York. (Bob Adelman/Magnum)

"*It was a devastating moment. After that there was a thing a lot of us went through, younger people who were involved, a period of guilt. We were shattered. It was then that we realized he was teaching, opening you up, helping you to develop. This was a brother you could believe. There was the sense that he was not in it for something. That was the extraordinary thing about him. He was in it because of his commitment to our liberation.*"—James Turner

February 27, 1965.
(UPI/Bettmann)

"I do not pretend to be a divine man, but I do believe in divine guidance, divine power, and in the fulfillment of divine prophecy. I am not educated, nor am I an expert in any particular field . . . but I am sincere and my sincerity is my credential."
—Malcolm X, March 12, 1964

1963 (UPI/Bettmann)

1919

May 10 Earl Little, a Baptist preacher from Georgia, and Louise Norton, of Grenada, married in Montreal, Canada.

End of World War I; First Pan-African Congress, Paris. § "Red Summer" in which scores of blacks are lynched and forced out of their burning homes; race riots in Washington, D.C., and Chicago.

1924

In Omaha, Nebraska, the Little family is threatened, as Malcolm wrote, by the Ku Klux Klan over Earl Little's Garveyite activity. Both Earl and Louise Little are organizers with Marcus Garvey's Universal Negro Improvement Association.

1925

May 19 Malcolm Little born at University Hospital, Omaha, to Louise and Earl Little.

Marcus Garvey is imprisoned on mail fraud charges.

1926

December The Little family moves to Milwaukee, Wisconsin.

1928

Herbert Hoover elected.

1929

The Littles buy a home in Lansing, Michigan. On November 7 the house is set on fire and destroyed. Earl Little builds a new home in East Lansing.

October: Stock market crash, onset of a world economic crisis.

1930

August: The First Temple of Islam founded in Detroit by followers of "The Prophet" W. D. Fard. This group will be known later as the Nation of Islam (NOI). § Ethiopia's Ras Tafari becomes Emperor Haile Selassie.

1931

September 28 Earl Little is run over by a streetcar and dies, reportedly at the hands of the Black Legion, a white supremacist group.

March 25: Arrest of the nine "Scottsboro Boys," Alabama.

1936

Franklin D. Roosevelt reelected; Jesse Owens wins four gold medals in the Berlin Olympic Games.

1939

January Louise Little is declared legally insane and committed to the state mental hospital in Kalamazoo, Michigan, remaining there 26 years.

Spring Malcolm Little is placed in a juvenile home.

World War II begins in Europe.

1940–41

Malcolm lives in various foster homes in Lansing.

February 1941 Goes to live with his sister Ella in Boston.

1940: FDR elected to third term; Richard Wright publishes Native Son. *§ 1941: U.S. enters war.*

1941–44

Malcolm works at odd jobs and for the New Haven Railroad, and gets involved in the Boston underworld. Moves to New York after several months in Michigan.

1943–44

October 1943 In New York, Malcolm is classified 4-F and disqualified for service in U.S. Army.

1943–44 Becomes more involved in hustling—selling drugs and bootleg whiskey—and gains the name "Detroit Red." Returns to Boston in 1944.

1943: Race riots in several U.S. cities; zoot suit and lindy hop sweep the country.

1945

January Malcolm spends several months working in local nightspots in Michigan.

August Takes up residence again in Harlem.

December Is involved in a string of thefts in Boston.

"Bebop" music, a new jazz sound, replaces swing as the music of the era; FDR dies, Truman becomes president. § August 6 and 9: U.S. drops atom bombs on Hiroshima and Nagasaki, Japan.

1946

January Malcolm is arrested in Boston on charges of larceny, breaking and entering, and possession of firearms.

February Begins serving ten-year sentence at Charlestown (Massachusetts) Prison, where he educates himself.

1947

January Malcolm is moved to Concord Reformatory. Converts to the Nation of Islam.

Jackie Robinson integrates major-league baseball.

1948–52

Malcolm is moved to Norfolk Prison Colony and back to Charlestown, where he finishes his sentence.

1949: People's Republic of China and State of Vietnam established; apartheid system established in South Africa. § 1950: Riots in Johannesburg against apartheid. Korean conflict begins.

1952

August Malcolm is paroled and travels to Inkster, Michigan, where he works as a furniture salesman. Goes to Chicago to hear the Honorable Elijah Muhammad preach.

September The NOI gives Malcolm Little the surname "X."

1953

January–June Malcolm X works at auto-assembly jobs.

June Appointed assistant minister at Detroit Temple No. 1.

Winter Named first minister of Boston Temple No. 11.

1954

March Malcolm X named acting minister of Philadelphia Temple No. 12.

June Named minister of New York Temple No. 7.

May 17: Supreme Court ruling, Brown v. Board of Ed. of Topeka, Kansas, ordering desegregation. § July 11: First White Citizens Council meeting, Mississippi.

1955

January: Notes of a Native Son, by James Baldwin, published. 60,000 blacks in South Africa protest forced removal from their homes. § August 28: Emmett Till killed, Mississippi. § November: South Africa leaves UN over issue of apartheid. § December: Rosa Parks refuses to give up seat on segregated bus in Alabama, setting off the Montgomery bus boycott.

1956

August 25–26 Malcolm X speaks at the first Southern Goodwill Tour of the Brotherhood of Islam in Atlanta, Georgia.

Montgomery, Alabama, bus boycott.

1957

Malcolm X founds *Muhammad Speaks*, the NOI newspaper, and organizes the Los Angeles temple.

April 14 Calms an angry crowd at 123rd Precinct after Nation of Islam member Hinton Johnson is beaten by New York police and jailed.

July 18 *Los Angeles Herald-Dispatch* runs an article and interview on Malcolm X.

October 30 Hospitalized in New York due to a possible heart attack.

January: Southern Christian Leadership Council (SCLC) founded. § March: Independence for Ghana. § August: Beginning of integration of Central High School, Little Rock, Arkansas. § September: President Eisenhower sends 1,000 soldiers to Little Rock to enforce integration.

1958

January 14 Malcolm X marries Betty (Sanders) X, a member of Temple No. 7, in Lansing, Michigan. They move to East Elmhurst, Queens (N.Y.C.).

November First child, Attallah, born to Malcolm and Betty.

1959

July Malcolm travels for three weeks as Elijah Muhammad's ambassador to the Middle East. Itinerary was to include Egypt, Iran, Syria, Ghana, and Mecca; he sent a letter from Sudan

1959

(continued)

during the trip, but he did not get to the Muslim holy city.

July 13-17 Mike Wallace's report, "The Hate That Hate Produced," airs on New York TV (and then nationally), bringing the first widespread notice of the Nation of Islam. Membership in the Nation of Islam booms.

December The family's second child, Qubilah, is born.

June 26: Prince Edward County, Virginia, abandons its school system rather than integrate it.

1960

September–October American Committee on Africa rally for Kwame Nkrumah, New York. Malcolm X debates Bayard Rustin at WBAI radio station, New York.

February 1: Greensboro sit-in, leading to sit-ins all over the South. § April 17: Student Nonviolent Coordinating Committee (SNCC) formed. Full independence for Sierra Leone. § May 6: Civil Rights Act signed. § June–October: Independence for Zaire, Somalia, Dahomey, Upper Volta, Ivory Coast, Chad, Congo-Brazzaville, Gabon, Senegal, Mali. § November: John F. Kennedy and Lyndon B. Johnson elected.

1961

March Malcolm X participates in a debate at Harvard with NAACP representative.

June 25 Leads Nation of Islam convention in Washington, D.C., attended by George Lincoln Rockwell and American Nazi Party.

August 27 Speaks at Nation of Islam rally, 369th Armory, New York.

October Appears on NBC-TV's "Open Mind" with Monroe Berger, Kenneth Clark, and Constance B. Motley.

Publication of C. Eric Lincoln's The Black Muslims in America. *§ January: Admission of two blacks to University of Georgia and subsequent riot. Congo's premier, Patrice Lumumba, assassinated. § Summer: Freedom Rides begin; bus-bombing and mob attacks in Alabama. § December: Independence for Tanganyika (later Tanzania).*

1962

January Malcolm X debates Bayard Rustin at a War Resisters League–sponsored debate in New York City.

February Malcolm debates Bayard Rustin in Chicago.

April 27 NOI member Ronald Stokes is killed and six other Muslims are wounded by police in Los Angeles mosque. Malcolm is sent to L.A. the next day.

May 5 Conducts funeral for Stokes, attended by more than 2,000.

July The family's third child, Ilyasah, is born.

October Debates Bayard Rustin for Project Awareness, Howard University.

December Rumors of Elijah Muhammad having adulterous affairs and six illegitimate children cause some Muslims to leave the headquarters mosque. Malcolm investigates the rumors and talks with three women who had served as Muhammad's secretaries and had children by him.

In South Africa, Nelson Mandela is sentenced to five years' imprisonment at Robben Island. § August: Independence for Jamaica, Trinidad and Tobago. § August 15–September 25: Eight black churches burned in Georgia. § September 29–October 2: President Kennedy federalizes troops in Mississippi; riot at University of Mississippi.

1963

January 11 Malcolm X leads protests at N.Y.C. Criminal Court over arrest of Muslims selling *Muhammad Speaks.*

Early 1963 Begins work on autobiography with Alex Haley.

February On several radio programs, Malcolm speaks about FBI surveillance and infiltration of NOI.

February 13 Leads hundreds of Black Muslims in Times Square rush-hour protest against police harassment.

March 23 Leads rally outside Micheaux's Nationalist Memorial Bookstore protesting violence against blacks in South, joined by Rep. Adam Clayton Powell and Dick Gregory.

April–May In Los Angeles for the trial of several Muslims resulting from the Ronald Stokes incident in 1962; heats up what is already a politicized trial.

Spring Relationship between Malcolm X and Elijah Muhammad and the Muhammad family deteriorates; Malcolm makes efforts to repair situation.

May *Playboy* publishes an interview with Malcolm X by Alex Haley.

Interviewed by James Baldwin on television.

May 12 Speaks before audience of 400 at a Washington, D.C., radio station.

May 17 *New York Times* reports he attacked President Kennedy over handling of Birmingham crisis.

May 25 *Amsterdam News* reports that Malcolm X attacked Martin Luther King, Jr., and other leaders for being unwitting tools of white liberals.

May 31 *Life* publishes "Black Muslim's Cry Grows Louder," by Gordon Parks.

June Malcolm X holds weekly rallies in Harlem addressing current issues and Muslim philosophy.

June 7 Attacks Los Angeles Mayor Sam Yorty and "KKK police force" in *Muhammad Speaks.*

June 13 Elijah Muhammad instructs Malcolm not to help civil rights demonstrations, according to FBI.

June 29 One of the largest and most widely covered rallies (the "Unity Rally") of Malcolm X's political life in Harlem.

July Appears at three-week demonstration at Brooklyn site of Downstate Medical Center.

New York Times reports Malcolm X is second-most-sought-after speaker for colleges (after Barry Goldwater).

Newspapers also report on Elijah Muhammad's infidelities with his secretaries.

August Malcolm announces that the Nation of Islam is not participating in the March on Washington.

August 28 Travels to observe the March on Washington.

Mid-September Appears at rally at 125th Street and Seventh Avenue in response to Birmingham bombing. Has to calm and break up a large crowd chanting "We want Malcolm X" after the other speakers talk.

November 10 Gives "A Message to the Grass Roots" at the Northern Negro Grass Roots Leadership Conference in Detroit, organized by Rev. Albert Cleage, Jr., in protest over conference given by Rev. C. L. Franklin and others.

December 1 Even though Elijah Muhammad had ordered ministers not to comment on the Kennedy assassination, at a rally in New York Malcolm utters the infamous line that it was a case of the "chickens coming home to roost."

December 4 Malcolm suspended from ministry and "silenced" by Muhammad for 90 days.

April–May: Ongoing demonstrations in Birmingham, Alabama. § June: Weeks of demonstrations in northern cities over discrimination. § June 11: Alabama Governor George Wallace defies integration orders. § June 12: Medgar Evers killed. § June 20: JFK meets with civil rights leaders to commandeer the March on Washington. § August 27: Death of African-American thinker and activist W. E. B. DuBois. § September 15: Bombing of 16th Street Baptist Church in Birmingham kills four little girls. § November 22: Assassination of President Kennedy in Dallas. § December: Independence for Kenya.

1964

January 15 Malcolm X and family visit training camp of Cassius Clay (later Muhammad Ali) in Miami.

February Malcolm refrains from publicly engaging in any Nation of Islam activity. A former assistant at the New York mosque tells him that a mosque official asked him to wire a bomb in Malcolm's car.

February 26 Despite Elijah Muhammad's wishes to the contrary, Malcolm goes to visit Cassius Clay again and is at Clay's world heavyweight bout with Sonny Liston. After winning, Clay announces that he is a Muslim and will be called Muhammad Ali. By this time he, like all other Muslims, was forbidden by Muhammad to speak to Malcolm X. They go to Harlem together, but soon after, their friendship becomes strained as Ali remains loyal to Elijah Muhammad.

March 8 Malcolm announces his break from the Nation of Islam and Elijah Muhammad.

March 10 The Nation of Islam sends Malcolm a letter requesting he vacate the house in East Elmhurst and return all NOI property.

Malcolm tells *Ebony* magazine that the Muslims can't afford to let him live.

March 12 At the Park Sheraton Hotel, New York, Malcolm announces the formation of the Muslim Mosque, Inc. in New York. Press conference also held at Micheaux's.

March 23 First speech after break with NOI, Hotel Theresa, Harlem.

March 26 Meets Martin Luther King, Jr., for the only time, at the U.S. Capitol.

April 3 Delivers "The Ballot or the Bullet" speech, CORE symposium, Cleveland.

April 8 NOI files eviction papers against Malcolm. He gives "The Black Revolution" speech at Militant Labor Forum.

April 13–21 Malcolm travels to Frankfurt, Cairo, and Jedda, according to FBI, under the name of Malik El-Shabazz.

April 20 Malcolm writes of the change that occurred within him at Mecca, moving beyond a black/white perspective to a more humanistic vision. Signs a letter detailing the changes he experienced on his pilgrimage "El-Hajj Malik El-Shabazz."

April 21–30 Guest of Saudi Arabia's Prince Faisal.

April 30–May 6 Malcolm travels to Beirut and back to Cairo and Alexandria.

May 6–10 Travels in Nigeria, speaks at University of Ibadan.

May 10–17 Travels and speaks in Ghana to the parliament, visits with Kwame Nkrumah.

May 17–19 Travels to Monrovia, Liberia; Dakar, Senegal; Morocco and Algeria.

May 21 Returns to New York.

May 23 Debates Louis Lomax on "The Negro Revolt," reports a shift in his attitude toward whites.

June 7 His new organization, Muslim Mosque, Inc., holds a rally at the Audubon Ballroom.

June 9 Interview on "The Mike Wallace News Program," reiterating a shift in views on whites.

June 16 Report in *New York Herald Tribune* that Malcolm is under police protection due to anonymous telephone threats.

June 26 Open letter in the *New York Post* from Malcolm X to Elijah Muhammad, calling for peace.

June 28 Malcolm announces the founding of the Organization of Afro-American Unity (OAAU).

June 30 Offers assistance to Martin Luther King, Jr., and to SNCC.

July 3 Reports a possible assault to police; officers posted outside house until next day.

July 5 Confronted by four men with knives outside his house.

July 7 Reports attempt on his life to police.

July 9 Leaves for four-and-a-half-month tour in Africa. Government surveillance kept up on Malcolm's entire journey.

July 17 Attends African Summit Conference, calls on the member African nations to bring the cause of American blacks to the United Nations. Organization of African Unity (OAU) denounces events going on in Mississippi.

July 18 Meets with Muslim educators, Cairo.

August 4 In Alexandria, Egypt, speaks to more than 800 Muslim students from Africa and Asia.

August 21 Attends second African Summit, Cairo.

September 1 Malcolm ordered by civil court in New York to vacate his Queens residence.

September 12 "I'm Talking to You, White Man: An Autobiography of Malcolm X" published in *Saturday Evening Post*.

October Student Nonviolent Coordinating Committee members John Lewis and Donald Harris run into Malcolm at New Stanley Hotel in Nairobi, Kenya, where they spend two days meeting. He criticizes civil rights groups for neglecting Africa. After this Malcolm makes several efforts to form ties with SNCC.

October 3 Speaks to 500 to 600 students, Addis Ababa, Ethiopia.

October 18 Flies to Kenya from Dar es Salaam with Kenyan President Jomo Kenyatta and Ugandan President Milton Obote.

October 29 Visits Lagos, Nigeria.

November 13 Leaves Conakry, French West Africa (now Guinea).

November 24 Malcolm returns from Africa, gives an interview denouncing U.S. policy toward Africa.

November 30 Travels to London for a debate at Oxford Union.

December The Shabazzes' fourth child, Gamilah, is born.

December 4 Minister Louis X (now Farrakhan) denounces Malcolm X in *Muhammad Speaks*.

December 12 Speaks at forum given by HARYOU-ACT (Harlem Youth Opportunities Unlimited and Associated Community Teams).

December 13 OAAU public meeting draws 500.

December 16 Speaks at Harvard Law School forum.

December 20 OAAU rally, Audubon Ballroom.

Late December Malcolm X speaks at a SNCC/MFDP rally in New York. Fannie Lou Hamer and the SNCC Freedom Singers come to a meeting of the OAAU, Hotel Theresa.

April 26: Mississippi Freedom Democratic Party (MFDP) founded. § Nelson Mandela sentenced to life imprisonment in South Africa. § June 21: Goodman, Schwerner, and Chaney killed in Mississippi. § July 2: President Johnson signs Civil Rights Act. § July 6: Independence for Malawi. § Summer: Mississippi "Freedom Summer." Riots in New York, New Jersey, Chicago, Philadelphia. Democratic convention, Atlantic City, New Jersey. § October: Independence for Zambia. § November: Lyndon B. Johnson and Hubert H. Humphrey elected. § December 10: Martin Luther King, Jr., accepts Nobel Peace Prize.

1965

January 7 Malcolm X gives speech to Militant Labor Forum, New York.

January 12 Checks into New York Hilton Hotel, under name M. Khalil, according to FBI.

January 19 TV appearance in Toronto, Canada.

January 24 Speaks at OAAU rally, New York.

January 28 Malcolm meets with two former NOI secretaries in Los Angeles.

January 29 Testifies before Illinois Attorney General concerning NOI.

Early 1965 Malcolm meets privately with some of the other civil rights leaders to iron out differences, talk strategy, and explain where he sees his program heading.

February 4 Invited by SNCC, Malcolm speaks at Brown Chapel, Selma, Alabama, during the voter registration campaign there. Martin Luther King, Jr., is in jail at the time and Malcolm speaks with Coretta King, saying that he wants to help their struggle.

February 5 Leaves for London.

February 8 Addresses the First Congress of the Council of African Organizations.

February 9 Flies to Paris but is refused entry; returns to London.

February 11 Speaks at London School of Economics.

February 13 Returns to New York.

February 14 Firebombing of the Shabazz home in East Elmhurst in the early morning hours. Malcolm flies to Detroit to make what will be his last major speech.

February 15 OAAU rally, Audubon Ballroom; 600 attend.

February 18 Evicted from home in East Elmhurst; moves household out.

Last speech, Barnard College, Columbia University.

1965

(continued)

Last radio interview, WINS, New York.

February 21 3:10 PM, Malcolm X, 39, is assassinated as he begins speaking at the Audubon Ballroom, dying from several gunshot wounds. Talmadge Hayer (aka Thomas Hagan) is arrested.

February 22 Elijah Muhammad denies that he or the Nation of Islam were involved in the death of Malcolm X.

February 23 Early AM, New York mosque burns.

February 27 Some 1,500 people attend funeral service held at Faith Temple Church of God in Christ in Harlem. Malcolm is buried at Ferncliff Cemetery, Hartsdale, New York.

February 28 Martin Luther King, Jr., speaking at Victory Baptist Church, Los Angeles, offers to "mediate the split within the Muslims" before further violence occurs.

March 11 A grand jury indicts Talmadge Hayer, Norman 3X Butler, and Thomas 15X Johnson for the murder of Malcolm X.

Shabazz family's twin daughters, Malaak and Malikah, are born.

November Publication of *The Autobiography of Malcolm X*, written with Alex Haley.

January-March: Marches and violence in Selma, followed by the march to Montgomery. § August 6: Voting Rights Act signed. § August 11–16: Watts riots.

1966

April 14 The three accused men are sentenced to life imprisonment for the murder of Malcolm X, after a two-month trial and despite testimony from Hayer that does not implicate either Butler or Johnson.

CONTRIBUTORS OF QUOTES

A. Peter Bailey, a journalist who lives in Richmond, Virginia, is working on several book projects. He frequently lectures on Malcolm X.

Chuck Stone is Walter Spearman Professor of Journalism at the University of North Carolina. He is a former editor of the *New York Age, Chicago Daily Defender,* and *Washington Afro-American* and was a columnist for the *Philadelphia Daily News.*

Louise Stone is the director of publications at the North Carolina Department of Labor.

William Strickland is an associate professor in the W. E. B. Du Bois Department of Afro-American Studies at the University of Massachusetts, Amherst. He is the former director of the Northern Student Movement.

James E. Turner is the founding director of Africana Studies, Cornell University.

ACKNOWLEDGMENTS

Much thanks for needed assistance, freely given, from Peter Bailey, Avery Brooks, Faith Hampton Childs, Claybourne Carson, Joseph Jarman, Louis Massiah, Attallah Shabazz, Louise and Chuck Stone, Bill Strickland, and James Turner.   —*Thulani Davis*

Photojournalists are not always aware that yesterday's pictures are the history of today or tomorrow. Those who contributed to this astounding collection of photographs of Malcolm X indeed do history a great service, bringing the dead Malcolm to life, illuminating his most provocative and productive years on the American scene.

Malcolm X was an amateur photographer and an astute observer of the press. He entrusted Robert Haggins, his personal photographer from 1960 to 1965, with providing an alternative to coverage by the white media, which Malcolm believed wanted to portray him as violent. The special access Malcolm also accorded *Life* photographer Gordon Parks is revealed in the private and public moments he recorded; Malcolm allowed Mr. Parks access to Muslim activities never granted any other photographer. Through her persistence in covering Malcolm and the Nation of Islam, Eve Arnold earned a degree of Malcolm's trust; he eventually granted her one of his earliest portrait sessions. Bob Adelman's documentation of the turbulent 1960s included Malcolm's participation in a surprising diversity of events. John Launois of Black Star was there to capture Malcolm's 1964 visit to the roots of Islam in the Arabic world. Henri Cartier-Bresson's portrait of Malcolm relates him to his mentor, Elijah Muhammad. Adger Cowans, Klytus Smith, O'Neal Lancy Abel, and Dr. Laurance G. Henry are African-American photographers whose individual photographs show us Malcolm the man as well as Malcolm the leader. *Life*'s archives provided us with isolated but important photographs taken by Truman Moore, Bob Gomel, Marvin Lichtner, and Ted Russell. AP/Wide World and UPI/Bettmann have once again fulfilled their mission in documenting the most newsworthy moments of our time.

Special thanks to Jim Huffman and Carla Williams at the Schomburg Center for Research in Black Culture at the New York Public Library. Thanks also to Patricia Lantis of Wide World Photos and David Greenstein of UPI/Bettmann Photos who allowed us access to their negative files to complete the record. We are equally indebted to Doris Fong of the Time/Life Picture Service, Ken Barboza of Black Images, Yukiko Launois of Black Star, and the Image Works for their cooperation. Thanks also to Leslie Willis of the Afro-American Historical and Cultural Museum in Philadelphia, and to Thulani Davis, Deborah Willis, Rebecca Williams, Mary Shea, and Michael Durham for leads in finding little-known photographs.   —*Howard Chapnick*

Designed by Jim Wageman

*The type for this book was set in
Janson and Gill Sans, composed
in-house on the Macintosh IIsi
in QuarkXpress 3.1, and output
on the Linotronic L300 at
Typogram, New York, New York.*

*The book was printed and bound
by Toppan Printing Company,
Tokyo, Japan.*

0860